HIDDEN RIVER POEMS

Allan Cooper

Acknowledgements: Some of these poems first appeared in *Atlantic Advocate, Dalhousie Review, Fiddlehead, Germination, Prism (International),* and *Skylight.*

Published by Fiddlehead Poetry Books, Fredericton, N.B., 1982, with the assistance of the University of New Brunswick, The Canada Council, and the New Brunswick Department of Youth, Recreation and Cultural Resources.

© Allan Cooper, 1982

Cover design by Alex McGibbon

Canadian Cataloguing in Publication Data

Cooper, Allan, 1954-
　Hidden river poems
ISBN 0-86-492-016-4
I. Title.

PS8555.066H52	C811'.54	C82-094891-8
PR9199.3.C55H52		

Contents

I THE PEARL INSIDE THE BODY

Equinox
Ghazal. In Memory of John Thompson
At Cleveland Brook
The Pearl Inside The Body
The Spirits Of Whales
Reptilian Calm
The Form
Black Holes
The Woman In the Blue Coat
The Moth

II HIDDEN RIVERS

The Starflower
Woman Listening
Poem For The Mother
Winds
Lifting A Rock
The Voices
The Gods
The Song
At Flat Brook

for Leigh Faulkner

A man faced with his own immensity
Wakes all the waves . . . .
                    —Theodore Roethke

whole galaxies spin
on the tip of a leaf

I

THE PEARL INSIDE THE BODY

EQUINOX

This first spring thaw
quickens me:

I feel the mole nosing his kingdom of dirt;
the brook-sound louder;

a bird settles
on a branch
        in the heart . . . .

    *   *   *

The words of the day gather like silt
at the edges of lawns.

For two days I have heard my voice
in the fir branch tapping against the pane.

Dark water overflows the road,
making the pavement shine.

I walk the air; enter the pale light
filtered through clouds.

    *   *   *

In woods, deer tread
on the sodden leaves.

I feel sap rising
like thoughts from a man
alone
for many days . . . .

    *   *   *

A richness rises from the earth:

*Bloodroot, buds swelling after rain,
the smell of musk in thick fir woods.*

*I walk a wild path across a field,
come to a place where waters overflow a bank.*

One leaf, still red, caught in a fissure of ice . . . .

*I look inside: the waters calm,
and the soul sings by itself.*

GHAZAL. IN MEMORY OF JOHN THOMPSON

In the afternoon I watch smooth brook stones:
gold, they overshine the sun.

The rare beauty of things: dark brooks;
and the voices of children, playing.

Where are all our books and stories?
Rest now, silent as a sleeping fly.

I hear your words; dark, they stir:
petals of a rose, growing from the unseen core.

I'll drop my hook in the water, raise
the great, grey soul, waiting in the shadow of that rock.

AT CLEVELAND BROOK

*Today I fished the brook again.
Standing on a granite stone
in mid-stream,
             I watched the brown trout
dart across the bottom of a rock pool,
into deep shadow . . . .*

*How long did I stand there —
the fishing-pole leaned against an alder,
the worms escaping from a can — wondering
at the mystery of the shadowy trout?*

*Years ago, my grandfather
walked these same stones,
fished this same brook.
How many of these brook stones
still contain
the sound of my grandfather's step?*

*And on a grey day, the grey sky misting,
how many still pools
give back the reflection of his face?*

*And how many descendants of trout
remember deep in their fins
the gleaming pearl of his sinker;
the pull of the line . . . .*

*Many dark grasses
have known the weight of the fishing-basket,
the slippery scales,*

             *the deep stain
of motionless trout.*

THE PEARL INSIDE THE BODY

— for Laurie
I am sitting at the kitchen table
eating toast and milk;
five years old.
           In a moment
my grandfather will walk
in through the woodshed
carrying a string of trout,
the dusk in his voice,
the sound of the brook caught
between his words.

    *   *   *

In the woodshed
there were always kittens
that slept in under wood
piled for winter burning.

  (The shed was lit
   by a bare lightbulb
   that swayed slowly
   as in wind.)

I remember them
chasing each other,
their shadow
on the wall

huge as the cat
my grandfather stalked
until blown snow covered the tracks
large as hands.

    *   *   *

*Christmas, 1959;
the house still dark.*

*I get out of bed,
a young boy
filled with the feeling of Christmas.*

*In the hall, my grandfather
stands in his long underwear,
the darkness
shadowy around him.*

*He tells me it is too early yet;
the house still cold.*

*I return to the bedroom,
my eyes
half-closed with sleep.*

*From the warmth of the bed
I can just make out
thin sounds from below,*

*my grandfather
striking a match.*

* * *

*The fall I was six,
my grandfather carried me
from the front porch,
around the house*

*to the garden
where cucumbers grew
in the heat of the sun
twenty summers.*

*I remember his steady gait;
the warmth in his voice;
the red hunting cap
blown off in sudden wind . . . .*

*He died in winter;
his voice rose
like longing
in my throat.*

*I carry it now
like a pearl
inside the body.*

THE SPIRITS OF WHALES

if the dream calls again,
if the voices rise like longing in my throat

and the dark crow wings
above the mountains of the flesh

and the mole noses this body of earth,
transforming molecule upon molecule

until each breaks free and breathes again
in open spaces —

I will come toward you shining,
neither sun nor moon

but like the spirits of whales,
waking all the waves.

REPTILIAN CALM

Earth clings to the edge of my dream:
where have I been?

The bat's erratic flight
enters my blood

On a still day, white clouds
sink to the marrow;

I feel them stir: a moon
slides through my veins

Neither is this the perfect dream:
wings rise from flesh

The dark, reptilian calm
settles in

THE FORM

At the side of the road,
there rises a form

almost human —
eyes like tiny stars —

its young hunched down
among freezing ditch grass

until the carlights recede,
the frog's slow croak returns

and the sounds of small feet
                              again
invade the roads.

BLACK HOLES

An air-raid siren suddenly sounds in the night;

*an engine plunges off a cliff, and the empty box cars
gather speed on the downgrade;*

the furnace explodes without warning;

*a supernova collapses in space, and its blackness
enters our dreams.*

Our bodies restless in the night,
filled with the dark
of an invisible moon

like a black eye watching,
    a dark energy revolving far out in space

drawing-in dream, consciousness, light

so that in the morning the body is like a fish marooned
    on the shore,
its grey scales drying in the relentless sun.

THE WOMAN IN THE BLUE COAT

I was waiting at a station of the blood
for the woman in the blue coat

who always arrives

she turns, smiles
enters a tree

or becomes the cat that haunts the house
where my great-grandfather was born

and always upon waking
there is a scent like blood
or balsam

    that lingers
even as I enter the street

THE MOTH

a man is lying on his bed;

the quiet of the room
broken only
by a moth tapping a bare lightbulb.

he rises,
and in one slow sweep
catches the moth in his hand.

wings beat soft as
silk against his palm.

he carries it to the window;
the night goes still

the dust from its wings
will mark him forever.

II

HIDDEN RIVERS

THE STARFLOWER

First week of May. The ants have begun their ancient labours; the grassblades are green with their lives. Cleaning the ditch, I put down the rake, and delve my hands deep into old leaves and grass . . . .

A starflower! — dry now, white — "the green gone out of it" — and yet still holding its form, like the veins of leaves . . . or like the design our own bones will make after death, cleansed of the flesh, slowly sinking into earth . . . .

WOMAN LISTENING

After heavy rain,
the trees bend in prayer
like a woman heavy with child,
listening inside:

How long the child has grown there,
a seed or bud,
eyes closed in womb-light,
feeling the placental rise and fall . . . .

She listens
with her blood
to the child

that now
begins its journey
through the earthy dark . . . .

POEM FOR THE MOTHER

Who is the mother
of all our days? — mother of light,
mother of joy, mother of fear-winds
blowing through the body . . . .

Secret source
that draws roots
to rivers in the earth —
we have known you

as longing surging through our bodies.
Mother, river
that carries us

sometimes we can almost see you,
as on a still day
a face seems to form in clouds . . . .

WINDS

*Winds that blow across the autumn fields
are great . . . yet how much greater
are the winds
that blow inside.*

*Listen to the sound
flowing from the breathing grass:
that same song pulses
in our cells and veins . . . .*

*Wherever we walk,
on hills, or in old pastures,
something is singing;*

*and the force of that sound
startles
the sleeping air . . . .*

LIFTING A ROCK

I lift a rock. Whose home is this?
Red ants quickly gather eggs;
the earthworm squirms
down his tunnel of earth . . . .

Such small lives! —
yet there are civilizations
beneath this rock; whole galaxies spin
on the tip of a leaf.

Our cities spread across landscapes
like the roots of trees . . . yet from the peaks
of mountains, even they are small.

Through the astronomer's eye,
even the largest galaxies
are tiny snail shells . . . .

THE VOICES

Even though the voices come toward us
over hills, valleys
and long fields, like the sound
of an approaching storm . . .

we continue to lie in our beds,
unaware of the opening door
and the shadow
falling across the room.

A god stands
at our shoulder, filled
with the essence of a sage;

yet we hear
only the sound of our blood,
the silence of our inner rooms.

THE GODS

*When the caribou dance
inside the old hunter
and we stand near streams, hearing
for the first time*

*the voices of fish and rocks,
and our own voices darken
as if nightfall and minerals
had entered them —*

*the gods will return
to hearths
and stone fences*

*and we will feel them,
like light
moving through stone . . . .*

THE SONG

Don't we sing the same song
again and again? — the one we learned
in our mother's arms, the first long cry of delight
ripening inside . . . .

And the trees, budding
with heavy rains,
don't they sing the same song? — and the ants,
performing their ancient labours.

We will carry the weight of this song
with us
to the grave,

intact, whole;
sound
entering the silence again . . . .

AT FLAT BROOK

*We approach; four blue herons
lift from the brook, into thick fog . . . .
The tide recedes along the shore;
light forms a nest in a sea-shell.*

*And the weight our bodies carry
becomes light
as a feather
falling from the tip of a heron's wing . . . .*

*We shout, and the sound
goes out across the water
like sudden joy:*

*The inner currents have been fed;
the herons fly on in fog
above the cliff . . . .*